BIRMINGHAM BETWEEN THE WARS

by

Joseph McKenna

The Council House Extension, 7th June 1926. Designed by Ashley and Newman, a London firm of architects, it was opened in June 1912.

Published by Birmingham Library Services and Hendon Publishing Co. Ltd.

Text and photographs © Birmingham Library Services, 1991

Printed by The Amadeus Press Ltd, Huddersfield, West Yorkshire, HD2 1YJ

INTRODUCTION

At the end of the First World War, Birmingham was the second city of the British Empire. It was three times the size of Glasgow, and twice the size of Manchester and Belfast. As the industrial heart of Britain, Birmingham was to play an important role in the nation's post-war recovery. Throughout the 1920s and 1930s, Birmingham reasserted herself both nationally and internationally, be it supplying a coining press to Tibet, railway rolling stock for Argentina or pipe-lines for Iraq. New industries such as electrical engineering and motor vehicle manufacturing grew. By the 1930s many factories were employing thousands of people. Firms began to move out of the crowded town onto new green-field sites in the country. Their labour force was drawn from the new Council estates, built in the outer suburbs. The mechanised motor industry produced subsidiary trades and encouraged the expansion of new industries such as rubber and non-ferrous metals. These new factories, with advanced technology, were able to ride out the worst effects of the Great Depression. In 1932, when the slump was greatest, only 14 per cent of Birmingham's population paying National Insurance, were unemployed, as against a national average of 20 per cent.

The City Council's immediate problem in post-war Birmingham, was to provide houses fit for heroes to live in. The Town Planning Committee calculated that it needed to build 2,500 houses a year just to fulfil its normal requirements. With backing from central government the City embarked on an ambitious housing programme. Vast council estates were built. When completed, Kingstanding had a larger population than Shrewsbury. Combined together the new estates had populations larger than those of Leicester or Plymouth.

The new estates were usually populated by younger married couples just starting their families. One of the most important tasks facing the Education Committee in the 1920s and 1930s, was the provision of new schools, particularly on these large housing estates. In all, 40 new schools were built between 1923 and 1935.

In 1938 the City celebrated the centenary of its incorporation as a Borough. The highlight of these celebrations was the Pageant, staged in Aston Park. Over 6,000 people were involved in this theatrical re-enactment of Birmingham's history. Added to this civic pride was the fact that the Prime Minister, Neville Chamberlain, was also a Birmingham man. 'Chamberlain the Peacemaker' he was called in 1938, the man who prevented war.

On the 21 December 1918, the Great War was over. That first peaceful Christmas in four years was a time for rejoicing. Here we see people queueing outside the premises of E. H. James of Dale End, for the first sale of whisky since the end of the war.

The Council House and Victoria Square, 7 June 1926. Designed by H. R. Yeoville Thomason, the beauty and imposing majesty of the Council House was not fully apparent until the demolition of Galloway's Corner in March 1970, thus affording a clear and unobstructed view. The statue in the foreground is that of Sir Robert Peel, founder of the police force. It now stands in front of the Police College in Edgbaston.

Victoria Square, 23 October 1925. The General Post Office, threatened with demolition in the early 1970s, has survived. Not so, the statue of King Edward VII, it now stands in Highgate Park.

Corporation Street, 22 May 1925. Driven through some of the worst slum properties of Victorian Birmingham, the street is 66 feet wide. It was begun in August 1878, but not finally completed until 1903. The Town Council very wisely retained the freehold of the land, and as the leases lapsed, large and valuable properties have come into its possession.

Corporation Street, September 1927, looking towards Lewis's and Central Hall.

Old Square, 9 March 1933. Some 700 years ago, the Hospital of St Thomas the Martyr or, as it was more popularly known, the Priory, stood on this site. The (Old) Square was developed from 1697 by John Pemberton, a Quaker ironmaster. Most of the original buildings in the Square were demolished with the cutting of Corporation Street in the 1880s. The building under construction to the left of the photograph is the extension to Lewis's departmental store.

King Edward Grammar School, New Street, 27 November 1935. The Grammar School was founded in 1552. The building shown here, just prior to demolition, was built in 1833-37, to a design by the well-known architects Charles Barry and Augustus Welby Pugin. In 1935 the school moved to a new 30 acre site in Edgbaston.

The construction of King Edward's House, September 1937. It was built on the site of the Grammar School, to a design by the Birmingham firm of architects, Essex & Goodwin.

High Street, viewed from Carrs Lane, looking towards New Street, 15 March 1932.

High Street, *c*.1925, looking towards Carrs Lane.

Marks & Spencer's store, situated at the corner of High Street and Castle Street, *c.*1930. This shop was built to replace the 'Original Penny Bazaar', opened by Marks & Spencer in 1904. On the night of 9-10 April 1941, the store was destroyed by enemy action. The present store was opened in 1946.

Old Bank, High Street, July 1932. The first Lloyd's Bank, then known as Taylor and Lloyd's,was opened in Birmingham on 3 June 1765, in Dale End. A blue plaque now marks the site. This bank, which faced Carrs Lane, closed at midday on 17 October 1942.

The old Bank of England, 17 February 1933. Built of Portland stone, the bank was situated at the corner of St Philip's Place and Temple Row, and was opened in 1890. It was the third Bank of England in the city. The first was situated in Union Street, and the second in Bennett's Hill. In 1967 the Bank purchased for a sum of £730,000, its present site at the nearby junction of Temple Row and Cherry Street. The old bank was demolished in February-March 1973.

Situated opposite the old Bank were numbers 29-37, Temple Row. It is believed that they were designed and built by William Westley, who drew the first authenticated map of Birmingham in 1731. This photograph was taken on 9 July 1933. These offices were demolished in the 1960s and replaced by Rackhams store, a building of limited architectural merit.

City Arcades, viewed from Union Street, *c*.1935. Designed by Newton & Cheatle, City Arcades were opened in 1902. There were three entrances: High Street, New Street and Union Street. *Allday's Directory of Birmingham* described them as 'bright and tasteful, being enlivened by the use of a light green faince in galleries, and like the older Arcades in the City, are well provided with shops of every description'. The section of the Arcades from New Street and High Street to Union Passage was completely destroyed in a bombing raid on the night of 9-10 April 1941.

Stevens Bar, 4 September 1932. A delightful little watering hole, situated on the corner of New Street and High Street. It fell victim to the dreaded and justifiably maligned, Inner Ring Road during the 1960s.

Edmund Street and Chamberlain Square, 1 March 1938. This section of Edmund Street between Congreve Street and Easy Row was cut in 1869. Up to 1879 it was known as New Edmund Street, being an extension of the original road, which took its name from a member of the Colmore family. Chamberlain Square, originally known as Chamberlain Place, perpetuates the memory of Joseph Chamberlain, who as Mayor, turned Birmingham into 'The Best-Governed City in the World'. The imposing building to the right of the photograph is Mason's College, forerunner of Birmingham University. The Central Library now occupies this site.

Easy Row looking towards Edmund Street, 30 August 1932. These Georgian buildings were demolished in the mid-1960s for the cutting of Paradise Circus.

The site of the Hall of Memory, July 1922. As early as February 1919, the Lord Mayor, Sir David Brooks, proposed the setting up of a war memorial to honour the memory of the City's 12,920 sons who fell in the Great War. In October 1919 the Council acquired, at a cost of £100,000, a large site bounded by Broad Street, Easy Row, Cambridge Street and Baskerville Place. In an open competition, which attracted 32 entries, the design for a 'Hall of Memory', by a Birmingham firm of Coke and Twist, was chosen. Their design was for an octagonal building, 35 feet in diameter, in bold Roman Doric. On 10 July 1922 work began on clearing the site.

The opening ceremony of the Hall of Memory. The City Council allocated £30,000 for the building of the Hall. The tender for its construction was won by John Barnsley & Son, with a bid of £23,000. Albert Toft R.A., was commissioned to execute four statues. One to represent womanhood, the other three to symbolise the Services. The foundation stone was laid by H.R.H. the Prince of Wales, on 12 June 1923, and it was opened on Saturday, 4 July 1925 by H.R.H. Prince Arthur of Connaught.

The Hall of Memory, 7 June 1926, with its Garden of Remembrance and Colonnade. Behind it the ground has been cleared for the construction of Municipal offices.

In 1934, because of overcrowding, the City Council decided to erect a new block of Municipal offices at the rear of the Hall of Memory. Three years were to elapse though before the Council gave its authority to proceed with the construction. T. Cecil Howitt was chosen as the architect, but due to the increase in the price of materials and labour, the original estimate rose from £259,550 to £344,040. On 27 June 1938, the Lord Mayor, Cllr. E. R. Canning, laid the foundation stone. The photograph shows the near completion of the East Wing of the Civic Centre as it appeared in July 1939. The war and the post-war recession halted any further development of the site. In March 1961 the building was renamed Baskerville House.

St Martin's Row and St Peter's Place, just off Broad Street, April 1938. St Martin's Row was so-called because a rope maker who had his premises here, made bell ropes for St Martin's Church in lieu of rent. St Peter's Place took its name from a Roman Catholic chapel opened here in 1783. Owing to the troubled times the exterior of the chapel was made to resemble a factory. It was only later that the turret shown here, was added. St Peter's was demolished in 1969 when the fabric of the building became unsafe. The Tudor-looking building at the apex of the two roads, was known as Stratford House. It was built in Victorian times on the site of the Three Horse Shoes, an inn which had stood here for over 200 years. At the bottom of St Peter's Place are the premises of Edwards & Sons. This building was formerly the Birmingham Brewery, opened in 1817. To the left is the Unitarian Church of the Messiah. This complete area has now been cleared for the construction of the Convention Centre.

The spire of the Unitarian Church of the Messiah dominates the skyline in this photograph of Broad Street, taken on 24 July 1934. Behind it is the turret clock of The Crown. It was here that William Butler, of the now famous Mitchell & Butler's Brewery of Cape Hill, first began brewing.

Five Ways, *c*.1934, looking towards Harborne and Edgbaston. The scene is dominated by the statue of the 19th Century political reformer and philanthropist, Joseph Sturge. The number 4 bus is making its way down Harborne Road to the village.

Snow Hill Station viewed from St Philip's churchyard, 29 March 1939. The pride of G.W.R., it was renowned for its cleanliness and efficiency.

Snow Hill Station, 15 January 1929. Opened in 1852, it was not until 1858 that the station adopted its present name. Previously it was known as Livery Street, or Great Charles Street Station. In 1871 the station was rebuilt, and the Great Western Hotel enlarged. Work began on further reconstruction in 1906, and a new entrance from Colmore Row through the hotel to the station, was built.

Bank Holiday crowd at Snow Hill Station, 1934.

An aerial view of New Street Station, 1928. The station, which officially opened on 1 July 1854, was originally known as Navigation Street Station. Begun in 1846, it took seven years to complete and was covered by a huge iron and glass roof, 1080 feet long, 212 feet in breadth and 75 feet in height. In 1929 L.M.S. considered alterations to the station. This brought forth a rather prophetic letter from a reader of the *Birmingham Mail*. He wrote:

> "Failing agreement to remove the station, it should be rebuilt at a lower level, and made an underground station, the whole of the top being covered over . . ."

New Street Station, November 1931. This was one of the busiest stations in the world. In one year alone, three million passengers bought tickets from here, some 190 trains entered the station and over 180 left. There were eight platforms and a staff of over 600 to maintain it.

New Street Station, November 1931.

Queen's Hotel, *c.*1925. The hotel adjacent to New Street Station, was opened in June 1854. It contained 60 bed and dressing room suites, a first and second class refreshment room, a large coffee room, and a smoking room. In 1872 the hotel was renamed The North Western (Queen's) Hotel to forestall a move by a rival hotelier, who proposed to call his hotel, just opposite the station, The North Western. The hotel was enlarged in 1911, and a new wing was added in 1917. The hotel was closed during the redevelopment of New Street Station in the 1960s.

Curzon Street Station, 19 August 1932. The station was the terminal of the London to Birmingham Railway. It was designed by Philip Hardwick and opened in 1838. The three-storey building with its giant Ionic columned portico, was a counterpart to the now demolished Doric porticoed entrance of Euston Station. The first train from London arrived here on 20 August 1838. With the opening of New Street Station in 1854, Curzon Street became a goods station, though it was used occasionally for excursion trains up to July 1910.

Steelhouse Lane Police Station, 10th August 1937. Designed by Herbert Humphries, the City Surveyor, Steelhouse Lane Police Station was formally opened on 4 December 1933 by Ald. W. E. Lovsey, Chairman of the City Watch Committee. The site was purchased in October 1923, for £12,500. Originally it was intended to extend Victoria Law Courts, but due to pressure from His Majesty's Inspector of Constabulary over the insanitary conditions of the existing police station, the Watch Committee relented. The new station cost £80,000 to build, and was constructed in brick and Portland stone, along 'simple Renaissance lines'.

The junction of Corporation Street and Aston Street, showing the Swan With Two Necks, February 1933. This is the site of the present Central Fire Station. Work began on the clearance of the site in July 1933.

The Central Fire Station, September 1937. Plans for the fire station were drawn up by the City Surveyor, Herbert Humphries, and the scheme was completed under the direction of his successor, Herbert Manzoni. The fire station was opened by H.R.H. the Duke of Kent on 2 December 1935.

Smithfield Market viewed from Bradford Street, *c.*1934. The wholesale vegetable market was built on the site of the former horse and cattle market in 1882-83. The buildings were enlarged in 1899 to cover the whole area between St. Martin's Lane, Jamaica Row, Moat Lane and Moat Row. The foundations fronting the last two named streets had to be dug to a depth of fourteen feet to get below the mud of the old moat. This site was formerly the home of the deBermingham family. Their name was perpetuated in the Birmingham Arms, the public house on the left of the photograph. This whole area is now covered by the present markets complex.

An early morning scene in Moat Lane, *c.*1934.

The Bull Ring, September 1937. The name dates from about 1750. Before this it was known as the Corn Cheaping, or market. It is traditionally the heart of Birmingham, and has long been a gathering place for the people. One of the more exciting episodes that took place here occurred one Sunday evening in 1758. A man named Morgan won a considerable wager by descending from the battlements of St Martin's Church, which is some 75 feet high, without the aid of a ladder or rope. He climbed down, by dropping from cornerstone to cornerstone. He was promptly arrested for his exploit, but was later released with a caution.

The Market Hall Clock was made in 1883 by Messrs W. Potts of Leeds, and was originally housed in the Imperial Arcade, Dale End. The dial was 5 feet across, 18 square feet in area, and weighed 15cwt. The largest bell weighed 3 cwt. The figures below represented Guy, Earl of Warwick, his wife, a retainer and a Saracen adversary. The two inner figures were seven and a half feet tall. In March 1936 the clock, which had not worked for 20 years, was repaired and installed in the Market Hall. On the night of 25-26 August 1940, the Hall was destroyed during an air raid, and with it the clock. Ald. Percy Shurmer, who was instrumental in the clock's installation in the Market Hall demanded that after the war a similar type of clock in Munich should replace it. 'They knocked ours to bits, lets have theirs to square it up,' he demanded.

Nelson's statue in the Bull Ring. This was the first public statue ever erected in Birmingham, and the first anywhere, to honour the naval hero. It was unveiled on 25 October 1809. Joseph Farrer, an auctioneer who lived in the High Street, bequeathed the sum of 6d a week to be paid forever out of the rent of a house in Bradford Street, for cleaning the statue and its base. The statue was removed during the construction of the Bull Ring Shopping Centre in the early 1960s, and re-sited in Moor Street.

Traffic congestion at the junction of High Street and Rea Street, Deritend, 15 May 1934. In the distance is Digbeth Police Station with its clock, and behind it the spire of St Martin's Church. The number 92 trolleybus in its Corporation livery, is one of the 49 Leyland six wheelers delivered in 1933. At this time the Corporation owned and ran the largest transport fleet in the world.

Deritend Bridge, 12 April 1932, looking towards Digbeth.

The Old Crown, 1931. With the death of Joshua Toulmin Smith in 1925, the 'Old Crown House' was put up for sale. At an auction held on 17 March 1925, the 'Crown' was bought by Holts Brewery of Aston for £5,000. G. H. Rodway was allowed to retain his half of the premises, which he ran as a restaurant, paying an annual ground rent to them of £92. In 1934 Holt's were taken over by Ansell's Brewery, and the Old Crown passed into their hands.

Anderton's Square, 4 September 1932. The Square was situated at the lower end of Whittal Street near its junction with Bath Street. It was approached by a narrow-arched passage and surrounded by a number of fairly substantial three-storey houses. The Square dates from the middle of the 18th century. The Whittall Street entrance to Printing House Street now marks its site.

Number 5, Bennett's Hill, 4 September 1932. Bennett's Hill was cut as recently as 1820, though the name goes back to the reign of Queen Mary Tudor. The naming of the road greatly upset Catherine Hutton, the daughter of Birmingham's first historian. In a letter headed 'Bennett's Hill near Birmingham', she writes, ' I say near, because an upstart of a street has arisen in Birmingham which has assumed the name of Bennett's Hill'. Miss Hutton was writing from the Bennett's Hill at Saltley, where her father had built a country house. The two houses shown here are situated near the top of the hill near its junction with Colmore Row. The bust above the window of number 5, is of the ancient Greek General Lysimachus.

Dingley's Hotel, Moor Street, 2 July 1933. The hotel was built during the reign of George II. One of its more colourful proprietors was John Milward, who it is said dined each day off silver dishes. Woe betide the guest who sat at his table without permission. It was said that he would keep the house empty rather than admit a guest of whom he disapproved. On one of the corner tables were some rather curious marks. They were the teeth marks of a strongman who was appearing at one of Birmingham's music halls. As a demonstration of his strength he took hold of this table by his teeth and lifted if from the ground. Milward died in August 1930, and his lovely old hotel was closed in the early 1960s for the cutting of the insidious Inner Ring Road.

St Bartholomew's Church, 29 December 1936. The church was built in 1749, on a site given by the Birmingham ironmaster, John Jennens. The architects are said to have been William and David Hiorne. In 1847 it became a parish church, although its parish was no more than 100 acres. The church became structurally unsafe and was closed in 1937. It was demolished during the Second World War, and the site is now used as a car park.

Ravenhurst, Camp Hill, 1931. The house was built in the mid-16th Century for Richard Smalbroke. In 1657, it, and the estate passed into the possession of Richard Lowe, whose family retained it for the next 150 years. In 1859 the house and almost an acre of land, was purchased at a cost of £1,700 by the Sisters of Mercy. Ravenhurst was destroyed by enemy action in 1940. St Anne's Roman Catholic Primary School, which opened in 1957, was built on the site.

A. B. Row, August 1932. Situated between Jennens Road and Belmont Row, Ashted, it derived its odd name because the corner house shown here was situated on the ancient boundary of the parishes of Aston and Birmingham. The stone above the door is inscribed with the initial letters of the two parishes, and below it is the date 1764, when the boundary stone was first placed here.

THE CORONATION OF GEORGE VI 1937

Colmore Row, 8 May.

Lucas's Factory, 5 May.

THE CORONATION OF GEORGE VI 1937

Ox roast at Harborne, 12 May.

Street party in Shakespeare Road, Ladywood, 12 May.

THE PAGEANT OF BIRMINGHAM 1938

The Pageant of Birmingham was a celebration to mark the 100th anniversary of Birmingham's incorporation as a borough. The pageant was held at Aston Park from 11-24 July, and traced the city's history from prehistoric times. 6000 performers were involved in the spectacular.

'Egbert' the Pageant monster emerges from the Pageant workshop in Cambridge Street.

Ancient Britons fight with a prehistoric beast.

THE PAGEANT OF BIRMINGHAM 1938

Archers in the Battle of Crecy.

Puritans, waiting their turn to go on.

The Town Hall, 1937.

The News Theatre, High Street, 1938.

St Philip's Cathedral, Friday, 1 September 1939.